STEAM MOTIVE POWER CENTRES

No.8: DARLINGTON

Including Darlington Works, Motive Power Dep

Copyright Book Law Publications 2008
ISBN 1-899624-96-6

INTRODUCTION

This album brings together the photographic work of Ian Falcus, Howard Forster and the late Frank Coulton who independently, between the years of 1953 and 1965, sought to capture and record the daily life of Darlington's passenger station, engine shed and locomotive works.

Both Ian and Howard began taking photographs in 1953 as teenage boys and journeyed from Heaton and Blaydon to Darlington on RCTS visits. During the guided tours (of the shed and the works) they meticulously documented locomotives in various stages of repair and being built at the works, the day-to-day servicing of a diverse range of engines at the shed and the comings and goings of passenger and freight trains at the station with their Kodak Box Brownies. Frank began documenting Darlington just over ten years later and his images portray a different era that incorporated former LMS and BR Standard locomotives leading towards the general run-down to the end of steam.

The closure of the shed and works in 1966 marked the end of a highly industrious period of steam locomotive construction in the North East of England. The shed was eventually demolished and the works site passed over for other industrial/commercial uses.

The images in this album have remained in personal collections, viewed by only a handful of the photographers' friends. In the case of Frank Coulton's' collection many images had never seen the light of day from the time they were taken up until 2006 - resting dormant for nearly forty years.

June 1957 saw the completion of a BR Standard Class 2, the last engine to be built at the North Road locomotive works. This year, just over fifty years later, work on A1 Peppercorn Pacific No.60163 TORNADO is moving tantalising close to completion and by the time this album is published it will have made its public debut. This album therefore offers a timely insight into the life and times of Darlington station, engine shed and the locomotive works in an era of renewed interest and rebirth.

With special thanks to Ian and Howard for the use of their collections and to Mark Williams for his technical assistance with Frank Coulton's' collection.

David Dunn, Cramlington. September 2008

(previous page) The general view from the southern end of the engine shed yard looking south on 9th May 1964. Darlington North signal box surveys the main line, whilst Bank Top station, with its three arched roof stands in the background. F.Coulton.

Printed and bound by The Amadeus Press, Cleckheaton, West Yorkshire
First published in the United Kingdom by Book Law Publications, 382 Carlton Hill, Nottingham, NG4 1JA

J21 No.65100 'brewing up' and ready to depart on the 11.00 a.m. Darlington to Penrith stopping train on Saturday 3rd October 1953. Note the wartime camouflaged cooling towers in the background and a uniformed schoolboy who would, in 2008, be drawing his old age pension. *H.Forster.*

Heading north on 19th August 1962, away from the station, V2 No.60945 has charge of a Down fitted goods whilst a DMU, arriving on a
4   local service, is nicely framed by the signal gantry. *H.Forster.*

On Sunday 31st August 1958 Longsight, Manchester based 'Royal Scot' No.46143 THE SOUTH STAFFORDSHIRE REGIMENT, departs for the south with the West Durham Railtour organised jointly by the Manchester Locomotive Society and the Stephenson Locomotive Society. Railtours became ever more popular as the end of steam loomed on the horizon. Later in this album we will witness another such tour reaching Darlington with some very unusual motive power bringing it from the East Midlands - the photographers surname is not meant as a clue to the name of one of the organising committee. During 1958 this 'Scot' clocked up more than 68,000 revenue earning miles, its highest since 1950 when it accomplished 68,454 miles. No doubt this rail tour would have contributed a couple of hundred miles to the total. *H.Forster.*

Also participating on that joint railtour of 31st August 1958 was Peppercorn K1 No.62059. The Darlington based 2-6-0 had not long since completed a General overhaul so its mechanical and exterior conditions were more or less assured. This engine had spent a three month spell at Ardsley during the previous summer but returned to the North Eastern Region thereafter. It was to end its days working from North Blyth shed and was condemned ingloriously due to accident when its slide bar and valve gear were mangled. Luckily, for BR, a scrapyard was just across the road so its movement to that place did not require too much in the way of towage fees. Note the spotters perched on their vantage points along the western perimeter wall of the station. *H.Forster.*

With its front end virtually sand blasted by dead insects, 'Top Shed' A4 No.60008 DWIGHT D. EISENHOWER is about to depart for King's Cross with an express from Newcastle on 19th August 1962. Unusually for a King's Cross engine, it appears quite dirty and, coupled with the fact that it had not long since received a General overhaul at Doncaster, its positively filthy! Perhaps Gateshead have had it for a few days or more and tried to get it looking like their Pacifics. Before its retirement less than twelve months after this view was caught, it would attend Doncaster for a month long Casual Light repair in January 1963. Thereafter, in preparation for its voyage across the Atlantic and subsequent preservation in the United States, it was given a quick restoration but not overhauled. Note the small party of junior 'spotters' watching avidly. *H.Forster.*

With at least 'twelve on,' A4 No.60030 GOLDEN FLEECE heads away from Bank Top with a Down express, passing beneath the newly erected footbridge to the diesel depot. The date is 13th August 1961 and the King's Cross Pacific is not long out of shops after a 'General' at Doncaster. Note the inverted train headboard which will no doubt carry the name of this engine's next southbound working. King's Cross footplate crews often carried these headboards 'between jobs' in this manner. On the footplate they would be a nuisance so what better place than that for which it was intended. *I.Falcus*.

On Sunday 19th August 1962, A3 No.60049 GALTEE MORE was photographed passing through Darlington's North Road station. The event came about because of engineering work on the ECML north of Darlington. The diverted A3 will take its northbound express via Bishop Auckland. *H.Forster.*

This image, taken en-route to the engine shed, manages to capture, although somewhat obscured by the fencing, the standby engine which on 27th March 1965 was Peppercorn A1 No.60124 KENILWORTH, minus nameplates. Note the proximity of the turntable which would be called upon to turn the 'standby' in a northerly direction if required. It was normal practice here to have the standby engine facing south. At this time the A1 was part of the diminishing Darlington allocation having arrived from York during the previous November. It would continue to serve 51A for another year when on 27th March 1966 it would be condemned and sold for scrap. *F.Coulton*.

Into the depot proper now, with the old roundhouse, which was not looking its best on this 27th day of March 1965, forming the backdrop. Locally based K1 No.62059 (some years on from and appearing decidedly different from the view outside Bank Top station on page 5) emerged from where most of Darlington's one-time large allocation of 'Austerity' J94 0-6-0 saddletanks used to stable. This building dated from 1866 and managed somehow to survive until 51A closed thereby reaching its 100th year of use. Behind can be seen the mechanical coaling plant which, until the erection of a similar appliance at Thornaby, was unique on the Region. Since its last picture was taken the K1 had helped out at Northallerton for five months in 1960. Its transfer to Blyth was some months off yet, just prior to the closure of Darlington shed. *F.Coulton.*

11

Wakefield based WD No.90116 stands outside the shed in superb ex works condition on 27th March 1965 after completing a 'General' at the nearby locomotive works. Waiting to return to its home depot, the 2-8-0 will have to undertake a few running-in turns before being released to traffic. Darlington shed had a fair number of WD 2-8-0s of its own for the freight workings undertaken but the extra three or four a week used on running-in turns helped to keep the number down. This overhaul was the last one given to No.90116 and for it to be given a life extension so late on confirms the usefulness of these excellent locomotives. *F.Coulton.*

Originally a Gateshead engine, and later transferred to Aberdeen Ferryhill, A4 No.60019 BITTERN is seen as recently out-shopped from the works. Ready to return to Aberdeen on 27th March 1965, this engine was one of six A4s to be preserved. Alongside the Pacific is another Wakefield based WD 2-8-0, No.90339, which had also recently passed through the shops Having been at Wakefield since becoming British Railways property in August 1949, No.90339 moved north to West Hartlepool in September 1966. Withdrawn in July 1967, just before steam was banished in the NE Region, the WD ended up at Drapers scrapyard in Hull amongst the throng of other Austerities purchased by the company during the final few years of their life. None of the 733 BR WDs were preserved! *F.Coulton.*

Neville Hill based, and ex works, Peppercorn K1 No.62007, buffered up to an ex works Stanier 8F at Darlington shed on Saturday 27th March 1965. Darlington works had been overhauling exLMS locomotives for a couple of years by now and although this engine is unidentified, as many as six a month were passing through the shops during this period of 1965. The K1 was coming towards the end of its running-in programme after a Heavy Intermediate overhaul but something was found to be wrong and it re-entered the works on the Monday morning for a week long Non-Classified repair. The power station cooling towers still show traces of the wartime camouflage some twenty years on. Beneath the towers BR had created a diesel railcar depot in the late 50s and a line of the resident DMUs can be seen standing outside. *F.Coulton.*

Reminiscent of the time when the Ministry of Supply wanted to off-load then, a line of redundant 0-6-0 'Austerity' saddletanks comprising, in order of appearance, Nos.68043, 68062, 68011, 68037, 68060 and 68023. The six J94 were stored at the south end of Darlington shed yard on Saturday 27th March 1965 as surplus to requirements but still 'on the books'. On the right, and hiding behind the brakevan it has in tow, a 350 h.p. 0-6-0 diesel-electric shunter crawled by, smug in its self sufficiency and effectiveness. On Sunday 23rd May four of the six 0-6-0STs were condemned and during the following day the other two in this line were also 'written off'. Local scrap merchants purchased the engines and they were hauled away to nearby yards. *F.Coulton*.

On 9th May 1964 Frank Coulton took this useful comparative shot of two different various styles of J94 bunkers. No.68051, on the left, carried the high bunker introduced by British Railways and this engine was the first NE Region J94 to be fitted (Gorton works initiated the extra capacity bunker programme in March 1948). That modification took place at Darlington works in September 1948 and over the next two years many more of the class had the additional sheet metal built on. No.68046, on the right, was still in its original condition with a normal bunker as purchased from the Ministry of Supply in 1946. No.68046 had route availability letters on the cab-side which were absent from No.68051. However, by this time trivia like that did not seem to matter and both of these engines were under sentence. Note that they are coupled together, pre-empting the decision and purchase which took place on 29th June when they were condemned. Their removal from Darlington shed did not take place until the following August when they were towed to a scrap yard in Middlesbrough. *F.Coulton.*

Another one for the modellers. A rear end shot of J94 No.68047 on Saturday 27th February 1965, showing details of its high sided bunker, ladders and footsteps. The 0-6-0ST is standing just outside the south entrance of the roundhouse with the straight shed and the ever present cooling towers behind. Note the good old shunters pole lay across the buffer and coupling hook. *F.Coulton*.

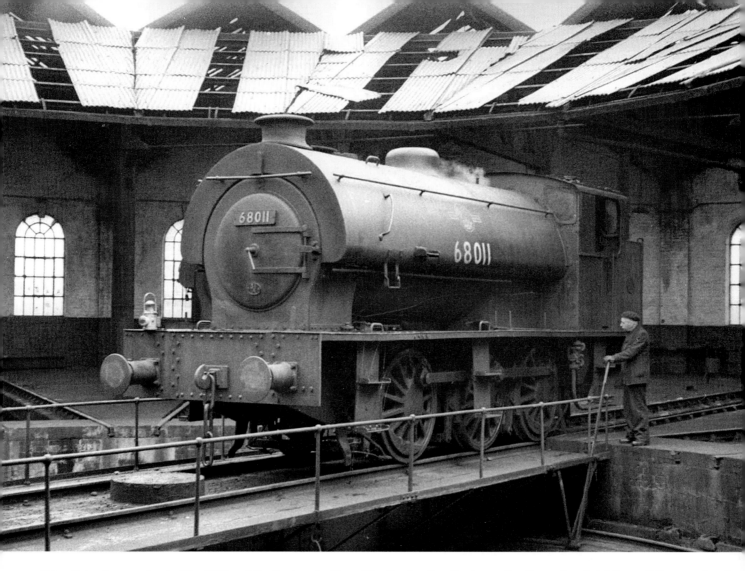

It is a Saturday morning in May 1964 and Darlington shed is putting its shunting fleet away for the weekend stabling - all its operational J94 saddletanks. This is No.68011 gingerly reversing off the turntable and into its stall to join others which are already 'tucked up' in the ancient roundhouse. One of the depot's disposal gang looks on nonchalantly as the rear wheels rumble over the gap in the rails. He also seems indifferent to or unaware of the precarious roof cladding right above his position (what price Health & Safety?). Open to the elements by now, the turntable once had a covering in the shape of a conical roof but that expired before the main shed was rebuilt and this cantilevered structure gave a semblance of cover to the front on the engines. Clad in corrugated iron, the fastenings have either rotted over the years or they were not too secure when first fitted; weather and pollution, besides the odd blast from a chimney have played their part in bringing ruin to the 'roof'. *F.Coulton.*

As mentioned earlier, Darlington works was, by the early 60s, maintaining a large number of LM Region steam locomotives. Consequently Darlington was sending them home in the Darlington style of how they sent their ex LNER charges home. Former LMS 'Jinty' No.47482 was out-shopped from the works during early May 1964 with North Eastern style numbers on the tank sides rather than on the bunker. On the 9th of that month the 0-6-0T was ready to return to its home shed at Crewe South. Ironically, this particular engine was used as a station pilot at Crewe - I wonder what the LM authorities at Crewe thought of this livery style? *F.Coulton.*

I was not going to include this shot of a locally based and very grubby looking Ivatt 4MT, No.43057, stabled at the north end of Darlington shed, alongside an equally grubby looking WD 2-8-0. However, poking out of the shed was something of a rarity in Darlington - an AC electric locomotive. The number of the Bo-Bo was not recorded but it appears to be one of the forty Doncaster built engines which became Class 85 (E3056-E3095). Its presence at Darlington on 26th June 1965 involved its inclusion in 'Torsion tests' being carried out by engineers based at Darlington. The tests required the use of the turntable situated behind the signal box at the south end of Darlington (Bank Top) station, where various electric and diesel locomotives were apparently placed with one bogie on the turntable whilst the other stayed firmly on the fixed rail. The table was then slowly turned to a point where tension was put onto the bogie springs. The results of the tests are unknown to this writer as are the other locomotive types involved although an English Electric Type 4 1-Co Co-1 may have been amongst those tested. As to why it took place at Darlington? *F.Coulton*.

In October 1956 six ex Great Central J10 0-6-0s were, on paper, transferred to Darlington shed. They travelled over the Stainmore route from their previous home at Wigan's Spring Branch shed. On reaching Darlington they were, after some delay in accounting procedures, withdrawn and then sent to North Road scrapyard for cutting up. The official date for transfer from the North-West to the North-East was 2nd December 1956 so a number of weeks had passed whilst the 0-6-0s lay dormant awaiting a drop of ink to be expended. Seen on shed on Sunday 9th December 1956 was No.65148 with the 51A shed code crudely chalked on the smoke box door. By now this engine was sixty years old and its five compatriots were of similar age. They never did any work from Darlington. No.65148 was condemned 10th December after entry to the works and then it went to the scrapyard at North Road on Saturday 29th December and was never seen again. *H.Forster.*

This view, captured from the coal heaps at the back of the 'dead line' on 7th May 1960, offered a panoramic view of the shed and yards at Bank Top. The building on the extreme left is the 1866 roundhouse with the dilapidated roof covering. Moving right the skeletal form of the mechanical coaling plant dominates the scene in defiance of the cooling towers on the right. The coaling plant was for many years somewhat unique in design and had been built in 1940 in time to handle the burden of wartime servicing.

Behind the coaler, and slightly to the south of it, can be made out the straight shed which was also a 1940 addition and which replaced a somewhat dilapidated NER shed of similar size and which also incorporated a wagon repair shop. The whole depot is a hive of activity, just as the enthusiasts of the day liked to see with comings and goings continually taking place. In the foreground though, two A8s, with only No.69858 identifiable, were on their way to the scrapyard at North Road. *H.Forster.*

The first A8 to receive the later (second) British Railways crest was No.69880 of Saltburn shed, shown here on Darlington shed on Sunday 12th May 1957 and recently ex works after receiving a General overhaul. Within weeks of the 4-6-2Ts return to traffic, diesel multiple units came onto the scene and rendered many of these engines redundant. No.69880 later moved on from Saltburn and transferred to West Hartlepool where it enjoyed working until June 1960 went it entered Darlington works for the last time and was immediately condemned. Shortly after this photograph was taken the big tank was in collision with an unknown adversary and had to go back to Darlington for a Casual Light repair which lasted from 24th May until 18th June. It was reputedly said that one member of the class, after a major overhaul, never turned a wheel in revenue earning service again. *H.Forster.*

It is Sunday 14th August 1960 and stabled for the weekend, before its running-in period begins after its first major overhaul since building, was New England based 9F No.92181. Fitted with a type BR1F tender, the engine is displaying the typically large numerals applied at Darlington works. Behind is a WD 2-8-0 which has also undergone a 'General'. Darlington did not overhaul many of these 2-10-0s, most being maintained by Crewe but they certainly made their mark on any 9F that did venture into the works. Entering traffic in November 1957, No.92181 was the fourth engine of the first batch of Swindon built examples. The tender, when fully loaded, weighed in at just over 55 and a quarter tons and was the heaviest of the BR Standard tenders except for the one-off BR1E (No.1271) used by 8P Pacific No.71000 (aka 'THE DUKE') from 1954 to 1957 and from then on by Midlands Line 9F No.92150. New England received the first eleven Swindon built 2-10-0s, No.92178 to 92188, and these added to the ten Crewe built examples which had also been delivered in 1957. No.92181 remained at New England until withdrawn in February 1965, not quite eight years old. *H.Forster.*

An immaculate broadside shot of a Tilbury based BR Standard Class 4MT tank locomotive seen on shed on Saturday 7th May 1960. Once something of a rarity in this part of the world, No.80073 was one of the Eastern Region members of its class which used to have classified repairs carried out at Stratford's High Meads works. However, when that establishment began its transformation into a diesel maintenance works, the 2-6-4Ts were sent for repair to the Old works at Stratford. But, entry into that particular factory was via a turntable which was ideal for 0-6-0 tender engines (uncoupled of course) but was a mite too short for these engines. So, from November 1957 the ER Cl.4 tanks made the long journey to Darlington for repairs. Most of the engines involved were based on the London, Tilbury, Southend section and Nos.80069 to 80080, 80096 to 80105, all took part in the trek and received 'Generals' at Darlington. In most cases these were the only General overhauls carried out on these short-lived locomotives. Nos.80133 to 80136 were given Intermediate overhauls at Darlington. To balance the work - for no workshop gave up its charges easily - Darlington sent its Cl.4 76XXX series 2-6-0s to undergo Stratford maintenance. Besides these ER engines, Darlington works also maintained the handful of North Eastern Region examples, Nos.80116 to 80120, which were shedded latterly at Whitby. Getting back to our subject here, No.80073, had just undergone a General overhaul. Its next repair was undertaken at Cowlairs after it transferred to Scottish Region in October 1963 but nothing major was done and nine months later it was condemned at Carstairs shed. *H.Forster.*

On Sunday 29th May 1960, two locomotives recently overhauled at the works stood on the shed yard looking somewhat splendid. J27 No.65875 was from North Blyth, and was probably waiting to return to the coalfields of Northumberland. BR Standard 9F 2-10-0 No.92184 was another of the Swindon built New England allocation which had also been given a major repair and it too was ready to return home. The 0-6-0 was some thirty-five years older than the 2-10-0 and would carry on working for another three years before a subsequent visit to Darlington works saw it condemned. With three transfers under its belt already, the 9F was to have three more before it settled down at Immingham but alas that was only temporary because in February 1965 it too was condemned simply because there was no work for it on the Eastern Region. The younger engine outlived its pre-Group cousin by less than two years whilst on the other hand some of the J27 class outlived most of the 9Fs - it was a funny time when head scratching became an everyday occurrence and the familiar question "What is going on?" was being asked everywhere. *H.Forster.*

Accompanied by other ex works engines, an A8 and a WD 2-8-0 amongst them, was Tyne Dock based Q7 No.63464 awaiting return to Tyneside on Thursday 16th May 1957. The 0-8-0 was actually released from works responsibility on the following Saturday 18th May but on Monday 20th May, it was back in shops again for adjustments and did not make its way home until the end of that week. The recessed spectacle plate was a rather unusual feature on these locomotives. Note the 'wrong facing lion' on the British Railways crest adorning the tender. *I.Falcus.*

In this aspect of the 'dead line' situated on the north-east perimeter of Darlington shed, you could be forgiven for thinking that the depot was in a semi-rural location but that was far from the truth. This splendid 13th August 1961 view of Heaton based V3 No.67647, awaiting entry to the works, reveals the NB lamp brackets on the footplate and NB destination board brackets above the smokebox. These were fitted to all of the V1 and V3 class engines when built. Further examination of the front end show rivets above the top hinge on the smokebox door where the GE Lines destination board brackets had been attached. *I.Falcus.*

Two weeks later and turning through nearly 180 degrees to his right from the previous illustration, the photographer caught this rather filthy Leicester based V2, No.60820, awaiting works and sandwiched between a Q6 and an L1. Examination of the inner edge of the footplate reveals the small splashers covering the coupled wheels. This engine was coupled at this time to one of the early Group Standard low fronted tenders. *I.Falcus.*

A long line of engines waiting to go to the works in October 1963. Sadly most of this lot were destined for the scrapyard and only J27 No.65832 (by far the oldest amongst them!), at the far end of the line, was to be repaired. The other engines comprised V2 No.60861 (Darlington built); British Railways 1949 Darlington-built J72s Nos.69004 and 69001; WD 'Austerity' 2-10-0 No.90763 which was one of a dozen of the class scrapped at Darlington and this engine was dispatched on 19th October; BR 'Clans' Nos.72001 CLAN CAMERON with 72003 CLAN FRASER, more remnants from the Scottish Region; V3 No.67682; and Darlington built BR Standard Cl2MT No.78012 from 1954 and, just in the picture, December 1953 built No.78011, all for cutting up. *W.P.Hodgson.*

Gresley K3s tended to be strangers on Darlington shed in the last decade of steam, however on 10th May 1959 No.61920, of Hull Dairycoates, turned up. For the first eleven years of its life this 2-6-0 was allocated to a number of sheds in the north-east, especially on Tyneside. Its last shed before going 'south' to Hull in July 1945 was in fact Darlington. Since the middle years of WW2 all K3 maintenance in England had been carried out by Doncaster, with Darlington concentrating on other classes. In September 1961 this engine entered Doncaster for the last time, was condemned and promptly cut up - another former LNER class which was soon eliminated from BR metals. *H.Forster.*

Here is a none shed subject but nevertheless seen from the depot precincts on Saturday 15th February 1958. Football excursions often involved interesting locomotive workings and New England shed sent this Thompson A2/2, No.60505 THANE OF FIFE to Darlington with a train of Peterborough United supporters. Having already turned for the homeward journey, and refuelled by the looks of it, the Pacific was seen passing Darlington shed with its empty stock. I'm afraid that the score of the match evades me for the moment but I am sure it could be recalled if pressed. This aspect gives a rather good view of the power station and its cooling towers which feature, prominently, in so many photographs of Darlington engine shed. Note also the newly established diesel multiple unit depot with its street lighting illumination. *H.Forster.*

33

The RCTS *East Midlander No 5* rail tour, of 13th May 1962, was hauled from Nottingham (Victoria) to Darlington (Bank Top) by Southern Region 'Schools' No.30925 CHELTENHAM, of Basingstoke shed, and LMS built 2P No.40646, which had been officially withdrawn from Bescot shed the previous day, but had been given special dispensation to haul the train. Having worked the train north via a number of unusual, interesting and freight only routes, the pair came off the train at Bank Top and handed over to an ex works WD 2-8-0, No.90348 which took the eight coach train on to North Road locomotive works. During that interval the 4-4-0s were seen on the main line with a rather young 'member' of the footplate crew leaning out of the cab and looking in the direction of travel. *H.Forster.*

Prior to working back to Nottingham with the RCTS special of 13th May 1962, the 'stranger in the camp', No.30925 CHELTENHAM was being inspected by interested BR staff outside Darlington roundhouse - why it was placed there is a mystery but not much would come out of that building during the weekend whereas the straight shed was busy all the time. Inside the building and elsewhere about the depot, three hundred plus enthusiasts took their inspection duties just as seriously, noting everything on wheels. The RCTS party had just visited the locomotive works and had been transported back over to Bank Top engine shed in a fleet of buses. Note the white painted buffer heads, a product of a night spent on Annesley shed. Certain areas of the locomotive appear to have been bulled-up whilst generally the thing looks moderately clean. The 'Schools' class and the RCTS have something of a history of course and a drawing of No.30925 appeared on the cover of every addition of the Railway Observer for many years, a fact that might have had some influence as to the chosen and most unusual motive power for this day out in Darlington. *H.Forster.*

Five ex Great Northern J50s were allocated to Darlington for different short periods during in 1958 and 1959. No.68897 was first to show up on 9th February 1958 from Low Moor shed. After sixteen months it packed its bags and went south to Wakefield. No.68934 arrived on 2nd March 1958 and stuck it out the longest at 51A, not departing until 2nd August 1959. It too had come from Low Moor but went to Ardsley. On 18th May 1958 three of the class arrived together in the shape of Nos.68898, 68909 and 68941, all from Ardsley. The latter was transferred to West Hartlepool a week later but the other two stayed on until June 1959 and went to Wakefield with the engine we can see here No.68897. The 0-6-0T is seen on 15th February 1958 in the roundhouse with A5 No.69841 for company, not a week after it had arrived from the south. *H Forster.*

A rear end shot of ex works, and York based Peppercorn K1 No.62065, showing details on the back plate of the tender, especially the electric lighting and associated conduit. The date is Saturday 9th May 1964 and the 2-6-0 had just finished a somewhat prolonged - six months - General overhaul with the inevitable running-in period and was ready to work back home. Apparently the engine was awaiting a boiler and eventually it got boiler No.29712 which came in with No.62060 in January 1964. However, No.62060 left Darlington works on 18th March 1964 with boiler No.29720 which had come off No.62065 - it seems there was more to it than a boiler repair. Buffered up in front was a tool van, above which can be seen part of the footbridge which spanned the mainline and led to the diesel multiple unit depot. In 1967 when many of this class was being sold for scrap, the accepted combined weight of engine and tender was 82 tons and 18 hundredweight for which scrap merchants at that time were paying British Railways £2,080. No.62065 went in March 1967 and ended up at Draper's yard in Hull, its cut up date was Monday 28th August 1967. *F.Coulton*.

On a cold 27th January 1965, BR Standard 4MT No.76110 of Dunfermline shed, awaits running-in following overhaul at Darlington works. By now Darlington was overhauling mainly ex LMS, BR Standard and WD 2-8-0 locomotives. At this time no less than fifteen Scottish depots had an example of this class on their books. Hurlford shed, where coal train haulage was the lot of their engines, had six of the class - Nos.76021, 76024, 76091, 76092, 76098 and 76108. Dunfermline had just two, this engine and 76109. Both of these engines had arrived in the Scottish Region new from Doncaster in August 1957 and went at first to Thornton Junction depot along with No.76111. From that shed the 2-6-0s worked passenger trains to Glasgow, Edinburgh and Dunfermline apparently replacing the LNER built D11/2 'Directors'. The move to Dunfermline took place in the early months of 1960 with No.76109 transferring in January and the other two following during April. No.76111 moved back to Thornton Junction in February 1962 but the others stuck it out at 62C where they found work on coal trains and trip freights. Dieselisation was fast becoming a reality in Scotland but many BR Standard Cl.4 tender engines hung on into 1966 and even u to May 1967, the official end of steam working north of the border. No.76110 went into store in 1966 and was finally condemned during December of that year. *F.Coulton.*

Although mainly found on the Southern and Western Regions, a small batch of BR Standard 3MT tank locomotives, Nos.82026, 82027, 82028 and 82029, were allocated to the North Eastern Region in the latter months of 1954. In numerical order, the first two went new to Kirkby Stephen shed in November 1954 for workings the Stainmore and Eden Valley lines, whilst the other pair went new to Darlington during the following December. On 22nd June 1957 No.82027 was at Darlington shed possibly awaiting repair but some six months later the 2-6-2T, along with sister No.82026, was to transfer to 51A at the start of a long migration which would eventually take all four of the NE Region allocation to the Southern Region by September 1963. By September of the following year they were all allocated to Nine Elms shed. During their time on the NE Region these engines were maintained at Darlington works, the only ones of their kind to go there for repair. *H.Forster.*

Darlington motive power depot had several engines of LMS design on its allocation, although this particular engine was actually built at Darlington in September 1951 - nearly four years after the demise of the LMS. Stabled for the weekend of 29th April 1956, Ivatt Class 2MT No.46477 was one of thirteen members of the class which were allocated to North Eastern Region sheds at this time and one of seven shedded at Darlington. Note the new 350 h.p. diesel-electric shunter on the right, 13242 (later D3242), one of over a hundred such diesel locomotives constructed at Darlington over the previous three years with many others yet to be built. Of the many hundreds of these diesel shunters which became TOPS Class 08, a very large number of the Darlington built machines failed to get their Tops numbers, being withdrawn shortly after the end of steam. Amongst the last batches which Darlington built, Nos.D4049 to D4094 appeared during 1961 and 1962 but by 1968 they were being condemned and sold for scrap; sixteen of that particular batch went before steam had finished. So it was not just the 9Fs which got a raw deal, so did some of the 'standard' diesel shunting locomotives too. What about D3242 - it ended up as 08174 and was withdrawn in August 1981 before going to Swindon where it was cut up during the following March. As for the Ivatt, well, hardly looking its best here, it was condemned in December 1962 after spending its whole life working from 51A. Spending nearly a year in store, for some reason, it was whisked into the works and cut up during January 1964. Its birth, short life and death must rate as something

of a record amongst steam locomotives by the simple fact that it all stemmed around Darlington. *H.Forster.*

A2 Pacifics of either the Peppercorn or Thompson variety were not normally seen on Darlington shed but on 13th May 1962, Thompson A2/3 No.60512 STEADY AIM, of York, was waiting to depart south. This engine was one of the longer lived members of the class because, along with Nos.60522 and 60524 it transferred to the Scottish Region in December 1962 whereupon they enjoyed another, albeit fitful, two and a half years work at St Margarets, Ferryhill and Dundee sheds. However, during their first months in Scotland all three were transferred to the former Caledonian shed at Polmadie of all places where, for most of the time, they were stored in a serviceable condition doing very little work on the main line south to Carlisle or beyond. Whereas the other two were condemned at 66A, our subject here went to Dundee Tay Bridge shed on 14th June 1965 but once again work was hard to find, even in more familiar territory. Withdrawal took place within a few days and A2/3 class ceased to exist from thereon. *H.Forster.*

Although only based a few miles away at West Auckland, the Gresley J39s were not regular visitors to Darlington shed in the latter days of steam, unlike in LNER days when at one time up to fifty of the class were on the allocation. On Sunday 8th October 1961, No.64848 appeared to be awaiting attention at the nearby works and in fact was accepted for a Casual Light repair a few days later. Throughout its life this engine had been allocated to sheds in the old North Eastern area but since the latter years of World War Two it had attended Cowlairs works for all its heavy overhauls. The LNER reasoning behind that was to share out the locomotive classes between workshops and, to some extent, keep the necessary stores in one place - NE and Scottish Area engines attended Cowlairs whilst the others in Southern Area attended Gorton or Stratford. That regime was adhered to during BR times but when the former LNER workshops were overloaded with back maintenance in the early fifties, Derby took on over two hundred of the J39 class and gave them heavy repairs. When everything had settled down and the status quo resumed, Darlington got a new role - cutting up a great many of the class as they were withdrawn. *H.Forster.*

On Sunday 8th July 1956 this Darlington based J77, No.68423, was idling away on its day off at the north end of the shed. Formerly, the 0-6-0T had been one of the numerous 0-4-4 Bogie Tank Passenger engines rebuilt to 0-6-0 tanks by the North Eastern Railway. This engine was converted at York in June 1902 and went to Middlesbrough shed from where it then worked for the next forty-six years. Note the Group Standard buffers, steam heating connecting hose and the vacuum ejector hose which Darlington had fitted in 1948. In October 1956 this locomotive was transferred to Haverton Hill where it managed to eke out another year of work before it was called into Darlington and condemned on 11th November 1957. *H.Forster.*

Fresh from the shops on 26th March 1961, Perth based V2 No.60970, awaited collection from the works crossing to take it to Darlington shed from where it would be run-in. At this overhaul, a Heavy General, a Smith speedometer had been fitted whereas as during its last overhaul, a Casual Heavy in March of the previous year, the engine had received separate cylinders, easily spotted here by the outside steam pipes. Being one of the longer-lived members of the class, No.60970 was given another 'General' at Darlington as late as January 1964. Just visible to the far left, behind the V3 bunker was an ominous sign of what the future held in the form of Type 2 and Type 4 diesel locomotives. *H.Forster.*

A busy but quiet scene in the works yard on a sunny Sunday 16th March 1958. This view captures the diverse collection of locomotives that were repaired at Darlington, and included are a couple of V2, a similar number of Thompson B1, Q6, J27, A5, J94, and in the left background, a batch of 350 h.p. diesel shunter cabs waiting to be fitted to another batch of Darlington's prolific diesel shunter building programme. In the foreground was the unusual sight of a J39. As alluded to earlier, No.64935 was an example of a type which were rarely repaired at Darlington; NE Region members of the class went instead to Glasgow but this Beyer, Peacock built J39 is in for a Casual Light repair which, in many instances, meant attention to collision damage. Neville Hill based No.64935 was to visit Darlington works twice more during the remaining years of its life; once for another Casual Light in February 1962 and then later in the year for withdrawal and scrapping. The townscape of Darlington - was that Hopetown - forms the backdrop to this picture. *I.Falcus*.

Saturday 6th October 1956 - Darlington works crossing. Selby based G5 No.67286 had arrived at the works during the previous day, for appraisal prior to undergoing repair. At the rear stands a WD 2-8-0 which was also awaiting inspection. On the following Monday morning the WD was accepted whilst the 0-4-4T was condemned and hauled away to North Road scrap yard. Still sixty years in traffic is not to be shunned - and it was a damn sight more than the poor old WD accomplished. The building behind the 2-8-0 still survives today, and is used as a garage workshop. *H.Forster.*

V1 tank No.67677 of Hull Botanic Gardens shed, in the usual photographic location by the side of the weighing shed on Saturday 6th October 1956. The smoke box numberplate and 53B shedplate had not yet been painted as that task was normally undertaken outside in the yard. The 2-6-2T had just completed a Heavy Intermediate overhaul and would return to Hull by the end of the following week after running-in. At its next, and final, 'shopping' two years hence, No.67677 would become a V3. This engine did not come to the north-east until February 1951 when it transferred to Middlesbrough from Norwich. In the twelve period from building at Doncaster to its arrival on Teesside, it had worked on the former Great Eastern lines from Stratford, King's Lynn, Parkeston and Norwich depots. Dairycoates became its last shed when it moved across town from Botanic Gardens in June 1959. Condemned there in October 1962, it returned to Darlington in February of the following year for scrapping. *H.Forster.*

It was always a thrill to see newly built or partially built steam locomotives on visits to main works. It seemed like an assurance that steam would be around for ever, no matter what the pessimists said. In October 1956 Darlington was still busy turning out new BR Standard Class 2MT tender engines of which No.78060 was one. Darlington built all sixty-five of the class and No.78060 appeared ready for traffic on 6th October. Stood next to two brand new BR3 type tenders - where are the last two - these must be Nos.1506 and 1507 with No.1505 coupled to No.78060. The last five of the Cl.2 engines, including No.78060, were off to the former Lancashire & Yorkshire shed at Wigan where they would replace a number of the ancient Class 'A' 0-6-0 tender engines. Of course the youthful ideals and optimism expressed earlier were well founded in that British Railways still had another four years of building steam locomotives in front of them - guaranteed! After that, well who could foretell the future? More 9Fs? 8Ps? *H.Forster.*

On another visit to the works crossing on Sunday 12th January 1958, Howard Forster found this one-time Selby allocated J73 No.68357, dumped and unfortunately withdrawn, awaiting haulage to the scrap yard. There were only ever ten J73 class constructed, all in 1891/92 and all at Gateshead. Their longevity is a tribute to their usefulness and the people who designed and built them all those years ago. No.68357 had started life on Tyneside and worked on both banks of that great river until a transfer in November 1937 took it to Humberside - Alexandra Dock shed to be exact. During the dark days of 1940 it moved up river to Selby and put in eighteen years of graft there. Due a boiler change in January 1958, it ventured up to Darlington but was instead condemned, one of three to go during that year. Alongside stood Heaton based V2 No.60835 THE GREEN HOWARD, awaiting entry to the works for a month long General overhaul. The V2's nameplate stands proudly on the running plate and so far it is still respected by all and sundry. This engine transferred to Gateshead in mid-June 1963 but by the end of that month it was sent off to earn its keep at Aberdeen Ferryhill. A year later it moved south but only as far as Edinburgh where it found residence at St Margarets shed for a fifteen month stay. Withdrawal took place on 19th October 1965 and two months later the 2-6-2 was in the hands of a scrap merchant. *H.Forster.*

49

Inside the erecting shop where new work was carried out, the last four BR Standard Class 2MT tanks to be built, Nos.84026—84029, destined for the Southern Region, were under construction on 31st march 1957. No.84029 remained at Darlington for quite a while, having been the last steam locomotive to be built at North Road works. All four initially went to Ramsgate shed but after two years moved inland to Ashford and from there to rapid decline. Two of the four, Nos.84026 and 84028 were sent to Eastleigh in November 1965 for possible use on the Isle of Wight but the decision was taken not to send them or the other eight members of the class which had been short-listed for export via the Southern Region works. *H.Forster.*

On Sunday 16th April 1961, B16/1 No.61416 was photographed standing alongside V2 No.60920 which was awaiting repair after a collision earlier in the month at an unknown location. The 4-6-0 carried a Mirfield (56D) shedplate and was one of a eleven of the class sent to the former Lancashire & Yorkshire depot in December 1960. The Mirfield B16s lasted less than a year at that shed and all had been condemned by September 1961. This engine, however, was already in works awaiting a decision which turned out to be negative and No.61416 was condemned within a month. The V2 did not fair much better and although it returned home to St Margarets shed in the July after this picture was taken, it was condemned in December 1962 and then cut up at Inverurie works in October 1963. *H.Forster.*

A smart greeting at the entrance to the Locomotive Department, North Road Engine Works - 27th January 1965. Where is that plaque today? *F.Coulton.*

The RCTS *East Midlander* from Nottingham to Darlington on the 13th May 1962, had unusual motive power for the short journey from Darlington (Bank Top) station to Darlington (North Road) prior to visiting the locomotive works. Ex works Wakefield WD 2-8-0 No.90348 did the honours and is seen en route to North Road passing the wagon shops. It was not everyday you saw a WD carrying express headlamps. However it is doubtful that the 2-8-0 exceeded the comfortable 40 m.p.h. limit at which these engines (and their tenders) started to make life difficult for the footplatemen. *H.Forster.*

A superb workshop study of three of the LNER's finest engines lined up in the main erecting shop on Saturday 27th March 1965. A3 No.60052 PRINCE PALATINE shows off the trough type Witte smoke deflectors at the start of a seven week long Casual Light repair. A4 No.60034 LORD FARINGDON looks particularly naked during its Heavy Intermediate, whilst V2 No.60824, having a Casual Light repair, still retains its coupled wheels. All three were now allocated to the Scottish Region, St Margarets claiming Nos.60052 and 60824 with Aberdeen Ferryhill keeping hold of the 'Streak'. There is order in this place amidst the barrows, jacks, vices and toolboxes. Come Monday morning and the noise of industry will return with a vengeance but not for much longer as Darlington's great days as a locomotive factory were drawing to a close. Note the works clock caught at 1.05 p.m. Memories! *F.Coulton.*

A3 No.60052 PRINCE PALATINE during its March repair in the main erecting shop. The yellow stripe on the cab side indicated that it was banned from working under the 25kV AC electrified wires south of Crewe! The drag beam, vacuum cylinder and injectors, are all visible beneath the cab. Staring us in the face with its sheen is a capstan and supporting ropes which were used to drag the engines in and out of the shops here. At the right of the picture, the ubiquitous wheelbarrow, which were found in these workshops in all shapes and sizes, would have been used to carry general wares around the works. *F.Coulton.*

Many of the locomotives 'scrapped' at Darlington did not necessarily pass through North Road scrapyard because this place, the Stripping Shop also took care of its share of the 'others' such as this former LMS 4F No.44301 ex Springs Branch, Wigan. Withdrawn during the previous March, the 0-6-0 was next in line for the chop and is pictured on Saturday 9th May 1964 sandwiched between a tender from an Ivatt 4MT and a tender from a WD 2-8-0, the engines of which had gone before. Why this Springs Branch engine should end up at Darlington is something of a mystery because sister engine No.44302, also of Springs Branch and condemned at virtually the same time, was sent to Crewe works for cutting up. Another Wigan 4F, No.44303 coincidentally, withdrawn six months before our subject here, was sent to Horwich for scrapping. The latter two incidences are quite understandable and made logistical sense but why No.44301 made such a journey to oblivion is lost in time. Perhaps it was failed whilst on a trip to the North Eastern Region with a goods train? Which explanation seems unlikely because Springs Branch had very few duties which took its 0-6-0s across the Pennines. Reasonable theories as to why this 4F came to Darlington would be welcome. *F.Coulton.*

Inside the main erecting shop on Sunday 17th January 1965 was Dundee based V2 No.60973 receiving a Heavy Intermediate overhaul. Nearly complete now but while awaiting coupling rods and lining, the 2-6-2 was attracting a lot of attention from the assembled enthusiasts. The anti-carbonising valve on the side of the smokebox was normally positioned on other engines with the shut off wheel at the front for ease of use, on the assumption that the majority of users would be right-handed. On all the V2s except 60800 Green Arrow, the wheel was on the left. Fitting the coupling rods would require that the locomotive be lifted and that the connecting rod be removed also, not to mention a host of other events which had to take place in a specific order to set up the whole thing properly. Preservationists know only too well the demands of setting up the valve gear on the simplest of locomotives but once three or more cylinders are involved! For the men at North Road works it was second nature. Darlington built, this engine had spent its whole life working from shed in Scotland starting at Haymarket in 1943. Dundee tay Bridge was to prove to be its final home and this repair was its its last. Nearly a year to the day after this scene was captured on film, the great engine was condemned and later sold for scrap. *F.Coulton.*

The front, workplace of the LNER Group Standard tender fitted to V2 No.60973, showing plenty of details. On the side can be seen the chalk guidelines for the lining - quite a refreshing detail at this time in the age of steam. Also the locomotive number - last three digits - on the coupling guide. Even the footplate floor timbers have been renewed but how long they will stay in that pristine condition is debatable. The electrification warning flashes are prominent with one either side of the coal door but the chances of No.60973 going 'under the wires' were minimal, however, better to be safe.... Note the Stanier 8F tender from unknown No.487XX in the background - also in for an Intermediate overhaul. *F.Coulton*.

Besides breaking up locomotives in the Stripping Shop, the place also carried out its normal function during the latter days of the works' existence - stripping locomotives ready for repair in the Erecting Shop. 'Britannia' No.70004 WILLIAM SHAKESPEARE was standing outside the Stripping Shop on Saturday 18th December 1965 but was thankfully awaiting light repair from a slight collision sustained in service. Already, by this time, a couple of 'Brits' had been scrapped so the Pacific was lucky to have ended up being repaired at all. No.70004 was the only 'Britannia' to be repaired at Darlington, the majority were handled by Crewe, Doncaster and Swindon. The other unique fact attached to this locomotive was that it was officially the last locomotive to receive a repair at Darlington. During the latter years of its operations, Darlington works could turn up virtually anything and usually did - if it was not already, it certainly became a very interesting place. *F.Coulton.*

The nameplates from V2 No.60835 THE GREEN HOWARD, were removed from the engine when a Deltic Type 5 D9008, took that regimental name in the Spring of 1964. Where the nameplates were removed is unknown because there is no record of the engine coming into Darlington works for the deed to be carried out. Was it done on shed and then the plates sent to Darlington by other means? Were both plates sent? Was it not usual at this time to present one of the pair to the organisation which the name represented? What is known is that one of the V2 plates was discovered at Darlington works lying face down in the mud, being used as a foot scraper. Note that apart from the dirt the plate is basically intact with all the necessary bits still attached. It was, apparently, very heavy to lift - 9th May 1964. *F.Coulton.*

Looking semi-smart on Sunday 26th May 1957 after its overhaul, Darlington based BR Standard class 3MT No.77004 languished outside the Weighing shed waiting for the necessary front end bits to be fitted and painted during the following Monday. The miniature snow plough had been fitted in readiness for its forthcoming duties working on the Stainmore line although snow was not expected till at least the end of November. A number of these engines were equipped to carry these small ploughs and those with the extra tall vacuum standpipe, such as that carried by our engine here, could easily accommodate the medium sized plough too. No.77004 was something of a nomad as far as engine sheds were concerned; during the twelve years of its life it managed no less than fifteen transfers, all within the North Eastern Region. During those moves it did manage to 'box the compass' with residences at sheds situated geographically at all four extremes of the Region. *I.Falcus.*

It is now 16th October 1956 and we are at Darlington works crossing to look at another Standard class 3MT in for overhaul, class leader No.77000 with one of the ubiquitous WD 2-8-0s maintained at North Road. The picture clearly illustrates the accessibility of the valve gear and pipework on these Standards' but their arrival on Britain's railway system was too late and all of the 999 Standards had very short working lives, some indecently so. The twenty strong 77XXX class had all been built at Swindon between February and September 1954. Allocated equally between the North Eastern Region and the Scottish Region, the first five went to the former, second five to the latter, next five to the former and last lot to Scotland. All ten of the Scottish based engines had been withdrawn by November 1966, a similar fate awaited the NER contingent but one of the them managed to escape to the Southern Region in March 1966 and worked from Guildford shed until the end of steam on the SR in July 1967. Two others kept going at York until June 1967 after which they ended up in a scrapyard at Chesterfield. Sadly, none of this class have been preserved. *H.Forster.*

A very interesting shot of steam locomotive tenders awaiting repair at Darlington on Saturday 26th June 1965. From front to back can be seen the tenders off A4 No.60010 DOMINION OF CANADA, that from a J27, a Q6, B1, another Q6, Ivatt 4MT and that from a 'Britannia'! Or was it a left-over BR1 from one of the erstwhile 'Clans'? To the left was a BR Standard class 5 tender along with Drewry and BR built 350hp diesel shunters. In 2005, I was able to walk through the A4 corridor tender, which is now in St Constant Railway Museum, Montreal, Canada. *F.Coulton*.

On that same Saturday in 1965 the frames from a withdrawn Ivatt Atlantic, which was dismantled in the scrapyard at North Road, still retained the Great Northern buffers and cylinders when utilised as a boiler carrier at Darlington works. The Ivatt 4-4-2 was one of nine C1s withdrawn at Doncaster during 1947 and which were then sent to Darlington for scrapping. The identity of the frames is unknown to this writer but it was photographed with a J27 boiler on board. Whatever happened to those frames I wonder. *F.Coulton.*

A long way from its home shed on 1st September 1957 but nevertheless within its natural home area, a Birkenhead J72, No.68714, was photographed at the works after having a Casual Light repair which commenced on 1st August. The 0-6-0T had been fitted with a short chimney in June 1948 to enable it to work under a low bridge on the Connahs Quay—Buckley branch. The Darlington built J72 had been shedded away from the North Eastern area since December 1930 when it transferred to Bidston in Cheshire. Over the following twenty-two years it was variously allocated to either Wrexham or Bidston, a sub shed of Wrexham, but in August 1952 went to Birkenhead. All of its overhauls during that period were undertaken at Darlington, with Gateshead used on one occasion in 1954, but this 1957 visit was to be its last to Darlington before withdrawal in March 1960. It finally came back to the north-east after thirty years work on the former Great Central system and was cut up at North Road. The reason for the large patch on the top of the smokebox was not known. In front of the J72, were the frames of a WD 2-8-0 awaiting a boiler. *H.Forster.*

Going slightly back in time - to 25th July 1954 - we find another North Eastern tank engine but one of much larger proportions than the previous 0-6-0T. Fresh out of the shops from a General overhaul, A8 No.69891 looked about ready to return to Middlesbrough after its running in turns. The route availability number was missing from the tankside but clearly seen, beneath the front end of the side tank, was the small operating rod for the mechanical lubricator. This engine had been rebuilt from a Class H1 4-4-4 in 1934 and since that time had managed to stay within the boundaries of Teesside. Its last shed was Thornaby but that was for a somewhat brief period of three months before it was condemned. Darlington called it in for scrapping in November 1958. *I.Falcus.*

On a cold and miserable 27th January 1965 the camera of Frank Coulton found Gresley A4 No.60011 EMPIRE OF INDIA awaiting the inevitable breaking up. Buffered up to No.11, and just out of picture to the right, was another withdrawn A4 No.60020 GUILLEMOT which had been at the works since the previous April. In the past, when all the A4s were in traffic hauling the premier express trains on the ECML, Darlington did not have much to do with the maintenance of these Pacifics, that particular role rested mainly in the hands of Doncaster 'Plant' works - their birthplace. However, as Doncaster gradually wound down its steam repairs it fell to Darlington to take up the reins with the survivors. During the final years of the rapidly dwindling class, Darlington managed to keep the engines going for further service in Scotland where they performed admirably. When Darlington eventually closed, the 'Streaks' were still working the Aberdeen—Glasgow 3-hour expresses but with their last place of maintenance gone, the A4's also called it a day. These two have already finished and would shortly be consigned to scrap. On the far left, just coming into the picture, was a brand new Darlington built Type 2 diesel-electric of the type which became Class 25. *F.Coulton.*

67

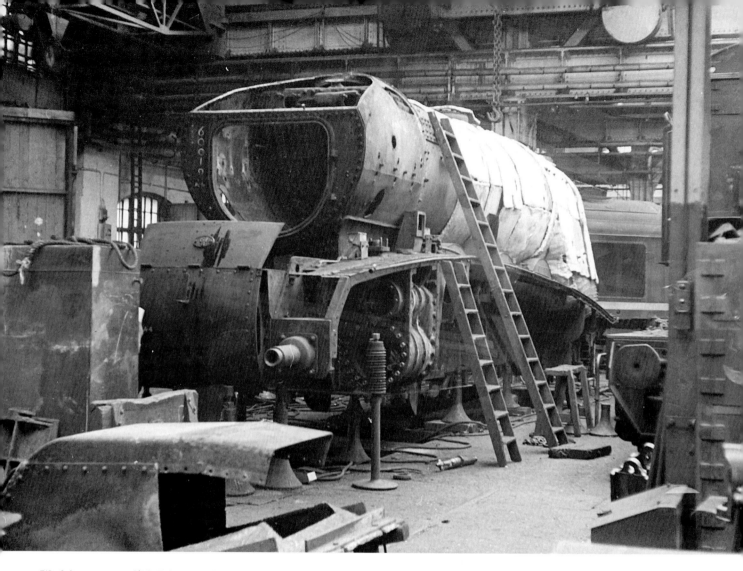

Work in progress - 27th February 1965 - the well stripped down carcass of A4 No.60019 BITTERN resided amongst a plethora of dismantled parts, ladders and tools. The Pacific is in the middle phase of a Heavy Intermediate overhaul during which it was to receive a refurbished boiler from spare stock. Visible were the Spencer double spring buffers, normally hidden by the streamlined casing. The weather was normal for a winter day - cold and gloomy - but this engine had no cause to feel the chill because it was one of the lucky ones and can still be seen to this day, preserved for posterity. However, it had to return to its place of work at Aberdeen Ferryhill to put a few more miles in before retirement called in September 1966. To the right, can be seen the bulkhead of a WD tender whilst beyond the A4, a Sulzer Type 4 diesel-electrics partially in view. Besides building the various diesel types, Darlington was also involved in their repair and maintenance so that anything from these large multi-wheeled monsters to the smallest shunters could be found gracing the premises. *F.Coulton.*

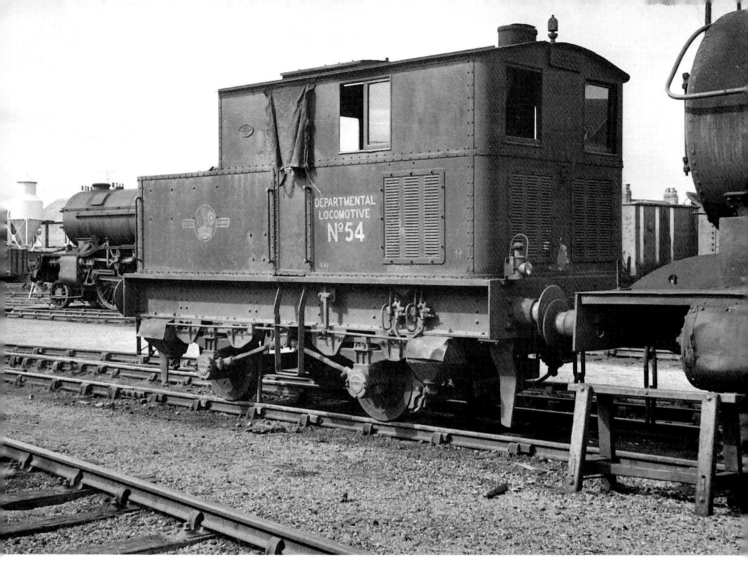

Departmental locomotive No.54, a Y1 class Sentinel formerly numbered 68153. Allocated to Darlington Permanent Way depot since new in December 1933, the four-wheeled engine was awaiting a decision on its future in the works yard on 13th August 1961. After withdrawal, during the previous June, it was sent to the scrapyard, then subsequently rescued to be sold into private preservation just three weeks after this image was captured on film. *I.Falcus*.

A very strange but nevertheless welcome visitor to the works in January 1965 was Langwith Junction based O4/8 No.63828. The 2-8-0 was attending Darlington to receive a Casual Heavy overhaul, its usual repair venue Gorton works having been closed by this date. Photographed on a cold and rather dull Wednesday 27th January, No.63828 had actually arrived nearly six weeks earlier on Tuesday 15th December but the overhaul did not commence until the 29th of January and its return to traffic was delayed until the end of February. In the event this 'shopping' turned out to be its last as it was condemned during the following August and later sold for scrap. This particular engine was not such a stranger as might at first be realised as it was actually allocated to Darlington shed during the first month of 1940 and had been in the LNER's North Eastern Area since purchased by the company in 1928. Its history records another major overhaul at Darlington as far back as September 1930 when it received a 'General' and a change of boiler. On the left is an orphaned WD tender whilst on the right the unmistakable stripped down A4 carcass is that of No.60034 LORD FARINGDON. *F.Coulton.*

Peppercorn A2 No.60528 TUDOR MINSTREL stands outside Stooperdale boiler shops awaiting entry to Darlington works on Saturday 27th March 1965. The absence of the front number plate and shedplate was rather strange, as the nameplates were still attached. It was more common at that time to see locomotives without nameplates but still carrying front numberplates and shedplates. The Dundee based Pacific had entered the works on 8th February for a Casual Light repair but it was not attended to until May and eventually returned to Tayside. In April 1966 it transferred to Ferryhill shed in Aberdeen but was condemned shortly afterwards and then sold for scrap. *F.Coulton.*

Gresley D49 'Hunt' No.62766 THE GRAFTON, a Hull Botanic Gardens engine, is on works on 12th October 1958 awaiting cutting up because it had been condemned on the last day of September. Perhaps the untidy removal of lagging around the exposed dome gives a clue as to why it had been condemned. The revealed asbestos lagging is also a poignant reminder of the hazards boilersmiths faced daily. Darlington scrap yard took care of most of this class in a process which took a number of years to complete. Photographs exist of D49s resident in the scrapyard at North Road still having their name, number, shed and worksplates attached. It would be interesting to see an inventory of the plates actually salvaged at the scrap yard and where they went from there. *I.Falcus.*